Contents

Foreword

A music education, especially one which opens the student's mind and ears to complex forms and idioms requiring focus and concentrated skill (like learning to play an instrument or singing), can take a lifetime's commitment, both for listeners and performers as well as composers. But it is a lifetime that is full of rewards, artistically, emotionally, socially and intellectually. Active engagement with music brings benefits throughout people's lives. Even very young children's perceptual development is enhanced by musical engagement, affecting language development, improving literacy and fine motor coordination. Participation in music also seems to improve spatial reasoning – one aspect of general intelligence related to some of the skills required in mathematics. While general attainment is clearly affected by literacy and numeracy skills, involvement in music appears to improve self-esteem, self-efficacy and aspirations – all important factors in improving young people's commitment to studying and perseverance in other subjects.

If music education is combined with the prioritising of creativity in young people the benefits are potentially huge. A creative mind is a healthy mind, and composing music is an unparalleled joy! I know – I speak from experience! From the first day I was able to share my musical imagination, in sounds I had created myself, with my friends, teachers and family, I had begun a life of creative sharing and inspiration. This can, and should, begin early in a young musician's life. Yes, of course on one level it involves a solitary and determined focus, but ultimately – and this is the key to the compositional instinct – it leads to a potentially massive shared experience, not just between the composer and their audience, but between the composer and their fellow musicians for whom the music is being written. There is palpable joy in this group work.

When the composer brings their ideas to the performing musicians, they are testing their decisions and possibilities in a public, rather than a private sphere. The ideas conceived in one's own silent thoughts are now out there, finding a practical and social application and context. It is a seminal moment, where the aims and goals of the individual transform into the aims and goals of the group. The composer is reflecting something of our shared humanity back to their friends and colleagues, and then on to a listening public. The communication is at once personal and social. The creative journey has involved an enhanced listening and will have developed, for the young composer, analytical skills and the making of decisions which will have an impact on the piece of music itself and on its receptive public.

The act of musical composition is a huge social and spiritual moment therefore, involving many people, reaching out from the creative subject to

Creative

Composition

for the

Classroom

by James MacMillan
and Jennifer Martin

Published by
Trinity College London Press Ltd
trinitycollege.com

Registered in England
Company no. 09726123

Printed in England by Halstan & Co, Amersham, Bucks

James MacMillan is the pre-eminent Scottish composer of his generation. He first attracted attention with the acclaimed BBC Proms premiere of The Confession of Isobel Gowdie (1990). His percussion concerto Veni, Veni Emmanuel (1992) has received over 500 performances worldwide by orchestras including London Symphony Orchestra, New York and Los Angeles Philharmonics and Cleveland Orchestra. Other major works include the cantata Seven Last Words from the Cross (1993), Quickening (1998) for soloists, children's choir, mixed choir and orchestra, the operas Inès de Castro (2001) and The Sacrifice (2005-06), St John Passion (2007), St Luke Passion (2013) and Symphony No.5: 'Le grand Inconnu' (2018).

He was featured composer at Edinburgh Festival (1993, 2019), Southbank Centre (1997), BBC's Barbican Composer Weekend (2005) and Grafenegg Festival (2012). His interpreters include soloists Evelyn Glennie, Colin Currie, Jean-Yves Thibaudet and Vadim Repin, conductors Leonard Slatkin, Sir Andrew Davis, Marin Alsop and Donald Runnicles, and choreographer Christopher Wheeldon. His recordings can be found on BMG/RCA Red Seal, BIS, Chandos, Naxos, Hyperion, Coro, Linn and Challenge Classics.

Recent highlights include MacMillan's Stabat Mater for The Sixteen streamed from the Sistine Chapel and premieres of a Trombone Concerto for Jörgen van Rijen, the armistice oratorio All the Hills and Vales Along, the 40-voice motet Vidi aquam, and Christmas Oratorio streamed in 2021 by NTR Dutch Radio from the Concertgebouw in Amsterdam. The annual Cumnock Tryst festival was founded by the composer in 2014 in his childhood town in Scotland.

Jennifer Martin is a composer who has spent much of her career working in music education; as a teacher and lecturer, an orchestral education manager and as a consultant.

Following her studies at the University of Edinburgh she was appointed Composer in Residence at Stewart's Melville College and The Mary Erskine School, Edinburgh, and teacher of Composition at the City of Edinburgh Music School, while also lecturing in the Animation Department of Edinburgh College of Art, in the Drama Department of Queen Margaret College and at the Music Faculty at the University of Edinburgh, where she taught both Composition and Music in the Community.

In 2003 she was appointed Learning Manager for the BBC Scottish Symphony Orchestra, where she was responsible for devising and managing a wide range of educational initiatives, both in Scotland and internationally.

Jennifer has developed creative education projects for the Glasgow Barons, Scottish Chamber Orchestra, Royal Scottish National Orchestra, Scottish Opera, Scottish Ensemble, Hebrides Ensemble, the Academy of St Martin in the Fields, Angus Council and The Cumnock Tryst, where she is now Chief Executive.

a wide group of receptive hearers. In educational terms it is an unparalleled lesson in the development of decision-making skills and learning confidence in one's own ideas, knowledge, experience and self-expression. Composing should be at the core of any musical education, regardless of where the young musician goes in later life, and music should be one of the basics of any person's well-rounded education.

Sir James MacMillan CBE

Acknowledgment

In writing this book, James and Jennifer gratefully acknowledge the wisdom and generosity of their own teachers, which continue to influence their work with young composers.

1 Why compose?

The sense of achievement inherent in creating something new;
self-expression; developing decision-making; developing critical thinking;
aural awareness; listening skills

Composition or Invention is now a major part of the music curriculum in our schools but there are also hundreds of young musicians composing on their own at home, experimenting with music software, developing their own ideas and sharing their work online without any help at all from their teachers. Most musicians start their careers by learning to play an instrument. We learn not only how the instrument works, but also how music works. We learn the 'theory' behind the music that we're playing – the pitches, keys, time signatures, rhythm and chords. We begin to understand what it looks like on the page, how it's written down, and then at some point we might think about writing music of our own. We might also be improvising, playing by ear, playing in a band or ensemble, and of course we will also be listening. Can any of us imagine a life without hearing music? It follows us around, through our headphones, in the car, in the shops, with every video we watch. It's everywhere!

There are so many routes into composing, but it's when we start writing our ideas down that we can begin to look at what we can do with even a tiny musical idea. And we can begin to understand how to use this language we call music to tell a story of our own.

There is no right or wrong way to compose, but there are techniques that we can learn to help make our music the most effective, the most communicative, or the most expressive that it can possibly be. Developing our ability to create, to self-express and to explore new sounds should be central to everyone's musical education. But to express ourselves through music, just like we express ourselves when we write a story, an essay or a poem, we have to learn the grammar of the language in the same way we learn to spell, use punctuation and write sentences. Composers spend a lifetime honing their musical language but it is often in our music lessons at school or with instrumental teachers where we set this learning process in motion.

So, why do we write music? Every composer will have different reasons but we might all have a few in common. It could be that we simply have so many ideas in our heads that they just have to come out. It could be that we want to tell our own story through our music, or we might want to express an emotion (love, anger, anxiety, joy) in a way that would be difficult to talk about or to write about in words. We might have to write a piece of music to pass an exam, or we might have been asked by someone to write a piece for a special occasion or a specific concert. And of course, we might just want to entertain our family, friends and a potential audience, whether they be online or in person at a gig or concert. It's always good to know the reason before we start our piece as it will inform what we do and how, and it will help us all the way through the creative process... but more on that later.

What skills might we need to write the best piece possible? Well, we need to be able to understand the basics of writing music down – especially important if we want someone else to play it or perform it in a group. It helps if we can develop our listening skills so we can start deciding what kind of music we like to hear and why, what music makes sense to us (or not), or why some music just doesn't interest us at all. We're all different, we all like different kinds of music, and it's really useful in this context to know what we like, why we like it and most importantly, how it was written. So, we're going to learn how to be musical detectives.

Another skill that we need to learn is that of critical thinking. This is when we have to decide what is working well or less well as we write our piece of music. Being critical of our work doesn't mean that we decide it's not any good and we should just give up! It means that we can say to ourselves that our melody really needs a different chord in the second bar because the harmony just isn't spooky enough; it means being able to tell when our piece is finished and really doesn't need those final eight bars; or it could mean that we decide to change one of the instruments because we're just not getting the sounds we want to hear. Being critical of our own work allows the piece to be the best that it can be. It's always a surprise when we hear our piece performed live for the first time and sometimes it's at that stage where we are most critical of our work and when we learn the most about how successful our piece is. As we learn more about composition – the techniques we need, the skills required – we get better at knowing what is working well or less well and we get better at thinking critically about what we have written and what we are hearing. Critical thinking allows us to find solutions to problems as they arise and it gives us the opportunity to sort them out. The more music we write, the better we become at knowing why our music is working well.

In our work with young composers over the years, both at university and college as well as in high school, we have noticed the steady advance of their computer skills, especially in the production of their scores and performing materials. There have been marvellous technological developments in related software which has become a useful and sometimes indispensable typesetting tool. However, technology can present certain drawbacks to the composer too.

There can sometimes be a temptation to use highly advanced technology as a shortcut in the compositional process where the software takes over from basic imagination. This is usually a mistake. The training of the inner ear – the way we hear and imagine pitches, rhythms, harmonies, durations, processes, structures – will always be of paramount importance for the composer. Software can't replace this natural musical function, and in the end will be of little help.

Software can sometimes also cut corners for a composer – and these are corners which must never be cut! Over-reliance on technology can have a deleterious effect on basic musical skills especially in fundamental matters like notation. A composer must learn the basics of how to get their ideas down on to manuscript. In this, the old-fashioned abilities come with the encouragement of 'paper and pencil' notation. This is where the groundwork has to be done. The composition student should feel the physical connection between inner ear, brain, hand, fingers, pencil and paper. There are no shortcuts. An understanding, knowledge and control of musical notation is a paramount and basic necessity for any composer.

Technology can then kick in to help the composer in the production of their materials or in some kind of recording of the work. But composition is a timeless and traditional craft and skill, involving a didactic process that takes time to build up. There are no shortcuts in learning an instrument, and similarly there are none in writing music.

Young people who find it difficult to express themselves in words can often achieve something very special through writing music. Watching your pupils moved almost to tears while they are hearing their music being performed for the first time, and knowing the sense of self-worth and intense pleasure that we can all attain through this medium, should never be taken lightly. When a young composer creates something beyond their wildest imagination, there is a sense of achievement rarely attainable in other areas of the curriculum. Music is a powerful communicator and the strength of emotion it arouses should never be underestimated.

Hearing what we have written is vital in our learning process. It allows us to identify any areas of weakness as well as the areas of strength in our technique. In the early stages of composing, it is through hearing that we develop our critical listening skills. There are often other musicians in a class for whom we can write, which will allow us to hear our work once it is completed. Schools also have a wealth of often untapped performance talent in staff and peripatetic instrumental teachers who can be brought in when new music is available for performance. Again, if the children see that professional musicians are taking what they have created seriously, and even performing it in public, the sense of achievement will be even greater.

We don't underestimate the problems of coordinating such events, but we can assure you, it is definitely worth it!

So how do we set up the environment of trust and respect within which young composers feel comfortable enough to express themselves in a new language? As music teachers, we are often dealing with smaller classes than in mainstream subjects, and we tend to have a healthy bond with our pupils, particularly in the upper years, because we are already making music with them. I would always suggest that, if we are asking our pupils to play, listen or compose, then we as teachers, play, listen and compose with them. I will always remember a teacher throwing her hands up in horror when I suggested that class teachers could write music alongside their children. 'How would we possibly have time?' she asked. Time is a good excuse, but we can work much more quickly than our pupils and even if we only manage eight bars, or an opening phrase, it shows solidarity with the class in what is a difficult task. It shows a willingness to put ourselves on the line. You will be surprised at what you will learn through composing, and have no doubt that it will feed directly into how you teach composition.

So how do we teach something that may have been a rare or problematic experience in our own learning, and what might make the process easier?

All aspects of music – aural training, analysis, history, orchestration, harmony, counterpoint, keyboard skills – can be taught and learnt through composing, and similarly we can teach and learn composition through these other elements. We have to identify suitable cross-over points and gauge what and where to overlap the various strands of the curriculum.

Teaching composition is more than teaching a technique. We are teaching a new language – a means through which a student can communicate something of their self. When it becomes a purely abstract exercise it will inevitably lose the enormous value inherent in the experience. We're going to give you some ideas on how to get the best out of your own pupils and, potentially, your own experience of composing.

2 What is this thing called music? Finding a common language

How we talk about music; developing a common language through listening; technical terms; musical intention

Creativity puts us, as individuals, on the line. We inevitably lay ourselves bare and expose something of ourselves to those who hear our music, and that can be a daunting prospect. But music is also a medium through which every individual can shine at their own level and in their own way, and it's often the simplest of musical ideas that give rise to the most direct expression or communication.

When we listen to music and analyse what we are actually hearing, we can define a common language, identify the ingredients required to compose a successful piece, and consequently begin teaching and learning the musical concepts often required for examination. The language we use to define this thing called music can be as simple or as complex as we require.

Here's an exercise to get the ball rolling, either with your class or on your own. The aim is to define a common language through a critical, aural analysis of a wide range of musics.

Write down in your own terms exactly what you hear when listening to as wide a variety of music as you can find. When you are looking for examples, ensure that you include both the familiar and the unfamiliar. World musics generate some of the more unusual timbres and rhythms while contemporary music deals with many of the issues of atonality.

Some of these could be useful to help get you started, for very different reasons:

1) **Laurie Anderson, *O Superman*** – shows how a single repeated element can act as the simplest constant binding ingredient around which melodies and other ideas – pictorial, literary, political etc – can be woven.

2) **Debussy, *Jeux*** – it's the web of tenuously connected ideas which could be fascinating for young minds: one motif seems to spawn the next, so that nothing ever returns in identical fashion. The music seems to defy rigorous analysis and that's why it would be very useful here! Hear the subtle interrelations of its themes, the limitless ambiguity of its structure/form and the endless fascination for ever-changing orchestral/ instrumental colours. We talk a lot about 'scoring' in our improvised games and this might focus the minds on how to continually imagine different combinations.

3) Stravinsky, *The Rite of Spring (Danse sacrale)* – this demonstrates the importance of simple repetitions, sometimes of the same one chord, or note, or sound. Also hear the excitement of irregular pulse groupings, and the way structures can be built up by juxtaposing and repeating tight little miniature phrases, keeping a tight control, self-limitation of material etc.

4) Schoenberg, *Pierrot Lunaire (Der Mondfleck)* – this work creates textures out of diverse lines, making a complex but unmuddied context where there is a lot of fast, busy activities, all operating together delicately. (Actually this is an interesting point to develop – hear the quiet, fragile phrases that don't need to be '*molto espressivo*' all the time.)
Also listen for the use of the voice (and text) in ways other than singing.

Here are a few more ideas, but really, anything would work well:

Denis Smalley, *Valley Flow* (Electroacoustic)

Rimsky-Korsakov, *The Flight of the Bumblebee*

Balinese Kecak (ritualistic chant)

James MacMillan, *Veni, veni Emmanuel*

Khatchaturian, *Sabre Dance*

Traditional Japanese, *Tamuke for Shakuhachi* (Bamboo Flute)

Xenakis, *Psappha for Percussion* (Contemporary Art Music)

If you are doing this exercise with your class, after each extract ask your students to read out what they have written and intervene with questions so that they have to justify their responses.

Typical responses might be:

I heard: background humming; a long whoosh; metallic sounds; a drum; it sounds like a bird soaring; it's really funny; it's like that dance New Zealand do before the rugby; there were voices; it had three sections; I could hear a bee; the music sounded far away; it was quite tuneful; it was really depressing; etc.

Useful questioning might be:

Did the background hum move up or down? Did it last through the whole extract? What was making the sound? Was it really a bee? Was it not an instrument trying to sound like a bee? What made the music buzz? What are the aspects of a bee in flight that the composer conveyed through the music? How did they do this?

A young composer's response during this exercise cannot be deemed wrong (unless they say cello when it is obviously a flute for example) and therefore everyone can add something to the discussion. What sounds like a bee to one person might sound like an engine to someone else, so we're also bringing a bit of life experience to the conversation. It is important to be positive about every response you get as we are already building the foundations of self-confidence in each composer.

So far, your students may not have uttered a single 'musical term' but you can now start to translate their ideas into defined concepts where appropriate ie. pitch, timbre, rhythm, dynamics, attack, articulation, structure, meter, canon, etc. This bank of words contains our building blocks for all subsequent composition. Our music will inevitably need to demonstrate some of these elements to succeed.

In some of these musical examples we can identify all of these main concepts, while others show only two or three. We can now begin to discuss what elements are essential when creating an effective piece of music.

We can also begin discussing the way music can be made to sound like something else: musical allusion. A bumblebee can be recreated with clever use of rhythm, choice of pitches and timbre. We can also be reminded of a place or event when listening to music: Mendelssohn's *Wedding March* for instance or *The Hebrides Overture*.

As listeners, we bring our own individual experiences to our interpretation of this language. Similarly, as composers we have to remember that if we are trying to communicate something quite specific to our listeners, they must have some understanding of the musical language we are using and perhaps even something of a common experience. *The Flight of the Bumble Bee* would be far less effective if we had never met a real, live bumble bee! If we had never experienced the swell of the seas around Fingal's Cave, would we fully understand Mendelssohn's experience of the Hebrides? The listener needs to understand something of our language to enable us to communicate clearly.

However, it must be stressed that as composers we should be prepared for an audience to take away something other than our original intention from our music. We are all individuals, and we bring such a variety of human and social experiences to our listening that we cannot be too prescriptive about what our listeners should hear or feel when they listen to our work.

So, we now have a common language, a bank of concepts, an array of building blocks, and are ready to create.

3 Let's create! Musical games and exercises

Games and ideas for classroom creativity; techniques to develop musical awareness; constructive criticism; starting points for composition

There are many musical games and exercises now in circulation to stimulate the creative or compositional process.

Games and exercises should always have a learning aim in mind. Knowing what we are trying to teach through them is fundamental to their success. Most of the games we will describe here are suitable for any secondary class and can be simplified for younger students or made more complex as required.

These games are best played with everyone sitting in a circle and with a variety of untuned percussion instruments in the middle.

Rhythm: 2-beat improvisation

Set up a pulse with everyone tapping their knees with their hands.

Example 1: 2-beat pulse

Once the pulse is established, instead of tapping knees each person in turn claps a new rhythm within that pulse. All repeat the new rhythm together.

Example 2: 2-beat improvisation, 2-beat repeat

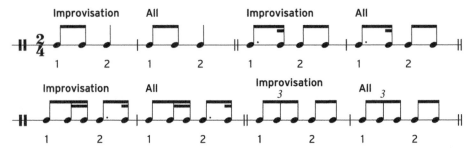

Try to keep the momentum: 2-beat improvisation, 2-beat repeat, 2-beat improvisation, 2-beat repeat. If anyone gets stuck, keep the pulse going by tapping knees again until they think of something.

Variations

- Use untuned percussion rather than clapping.

- Using a variety of untuned percussion, only those with an instrument of the same family as the soloist should repeat the new rhythm. For example, if the new rhythm is played on a metal instrument, then only metal instruments repeat. Similarly with wood, skins or shakers.

- Experiment with different dynamics, possibly relating to families of percussion instruments, ie anyone playing a metal instrument has to play very softly, anyone with a tambourine has to play really loudly, etc.

- Extend the number of beats for the improvisation to three, four or five:

Example 3: Improvisation in $\frac{3}{4}$

Example 4: Improvisation in $\frac{4}{4}$

Example 5: Improvisation in $\frac{5}{4}$

Sing a phrase to any vowel sound for example, instead of clapping.

Example 6: Improvisation on a vowel

Example 7: Improvisation on a vowel

Starting point for composition

Getting started is often the most difficult part of writing music. Finding an idea that sparks us off can take time. Through improvisation, we create something very quickly and spontaneously. It is a good idea for a teacher to record such exercises so that an individual student can hear their contribution and develop it once the game is long forgotten. Even a 2-beat rhythm can be developed, and if coupled further to 2-beat cells, we have the beginnings of something quite substantial.

Let a student experiment with fitting four cells together in different orders. The following cells contain the types of rhythms which will be created in the first exercise above. Let the students write these rhythms down as it's good practice. The more they notate at this stage themselves the better, and the more hands-on they become with their musical material.

Example 8: 2-beat cells

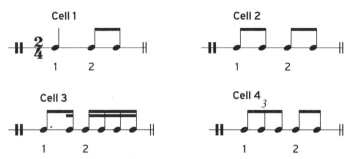

Now put them in any order. Don't think too hard about it. Just mix them up and then try playing them to see if they sound good. You could print out multiple, large copies of four cells and put them on the floor or on a desk in different combinations so that a group can play through them together. For example:

Example 9: 2-beat cell combinations

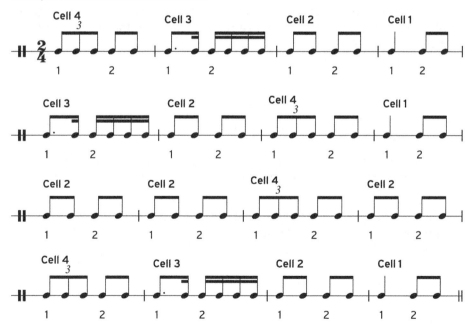

Always ensure that the results of an exercise like this are actually played so that your students can hear whether it works as a piece of music and can therefore make decisions as to what can be kept and what needs to be changed. This is the start of critical listening. If the cells don't sound good, change them. If the order doesn't work, change it.

What happens if the rhythms of these cells are reversed?

Example 10: 2-beat cells reversed

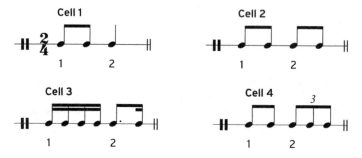

There are now seven different cells to play with. (Cell 2 is obviously the same forwards and backwards.) Add these retrograde cells into the pot of cells to choose from.

Variations

- Try playing different cells with a different timbre of percussion instrument ie cell 1 forwards or backwards is played on metals; cell 2 forwards or backwards is always played on drums etc.

- Try layering the rhythms. A good way to explore this is for one group to start playing the 'piece' and then another group joins in two bars later creating a rhythmic canon.

- You could write a piece for four separate percussion instruments using only four rhythmic cells, for example:

Example 11: Percussion piece based on 4 rhythmic cells

Using some of these ideas, see where your students could take this piece. How could they develop it? How could the ideas evolve? Ask them to write another 8 or 16 bars and then play the results. Choose instruments available in the class so that they can hear the results. How fast should it go? Think about the range of dynamics available. Look at articulation. It's the detail that makes a repeating pattern sound interesting and gives it a sense of direction and purpose.

- How could a rhythm be developed through augmentation or diminution?

Example 12: Cell development

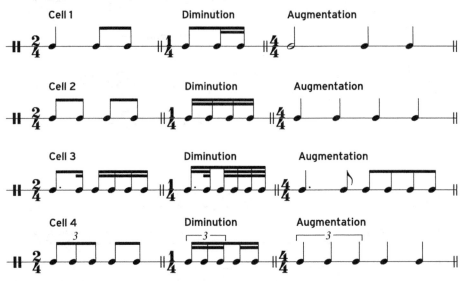

- Could you add some of these new versions to the originals in a development section?

- What happens if you add a quaver to the bar length or take a quaver away?

Example 13: Altering cell lengths

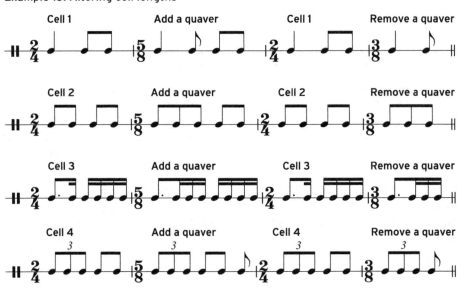

We now have a substantial amount of material which could easily be put together into a piece for untuned percussion.

Example 14: Percussion piece using material developed so far

Word samba

Split the class into five groups. Each group will be responsible for keeping one rhythm going. Start with the basic pulse and add groups to the ensemble. The result is a complex vocal samba.

Example 15: Word samba

Variations

- Once everyone is confident with saying the rhythms, play them on untuned percussion instead. Group 1 on drums, Group 2 on maracas etc. Students can choose which rhythms to play on each family of instruments.

- Experiment with dynamic changes.

- Make up further rhythms from nonsense text, transferring them on to percussion instruments.

- Add pitched instruments (in C major). Change from chord I to V for the fourth beat or from chord I to V every fourth quaver.

Speech rhythm and intonation

Say a simple phrase to the class using the natural intonation and rhythm of the words. Let them all repeat it, copying your speech rhythm and intonation as closely as possible. The phrase *'My name is...'* is useful for this one. An approximation of speaking this phrase could be notated as:

Example 16: Notating speech

'Good Morning' or *'I've been to...'* are also good phrases to try. Each student can add their own spoken phrase in turn and all then repeat. Try a variety of outlandish modes of speaking, and encourage careful and attentive listening so that students can repeat what each has said as accurately as possible.

Variations

- Say a simple phrase to the class and let them play the rhythm of the spoken text back to you on simple percussion. Set up a spoken/played conversation.

Example 17: Speech and percussion conversation

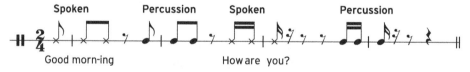

- Develop this by splitting into pairs and improvising a rhythmic conversation with no words this time, but complete with dynamics and speed changes. The aim is to express an imaginary sentence as fully as possible. So decide in pairs what you want to 'discuss'. Each pair then uses a combination of percussion timbres (eg wood/metal, or skin/wood) or clap depending on what their conversation was about.

If these conversations are performed to the rest of the class, check to see whether the sentiment of the conversation was communicated clearly and indeed whether each person in the pair had the same sentiment in mind when musically conversing! It is useful to talk about which musical elements helped or hindered the audience's understanding.

This exercise could be used with any age group as the musical outcomes will be as simple or as complex as the musical knowledge of those involved. The most important thing is to keep it 'musical' with each player maintaining rhythmic clarity, a sense of direction through dynamic contrast and a clear sense of intention or communication. And of course, all of these improvisations can be recorded, notated and then used as the starting points of a new piece.

It is important to reiterate the whole idea of 'music as language' with an exercise like this. What do we need to have in common with our audience to communicate succinctly? What musical concepts made you think that a timid, quiet musical conversation was communicating fear and trembling? Some modes of playing will communicate the same feelings to most of us, but it doesn't work like that all the time. The more musical parameters we include, the more chance we have of communicating something more rigorously. If we include tortured, chromatic harmonies to our timid and quiet conversation for instance, the feelings of fear and dread could be accentuated further.

Starting point for composition

The idea of using speech rhythm and intonation as a starting point for composition is not new. Janáček painstakingly notated the natural rising and falling of pitch and the rhythms of the spoken word. If a student is setting a text, always suggest they look at, and identify, its own rhythms and melody as a way of getting started.

Pitch

Have the class sit in a circle. Ask them all to breathe in slowly and then exhale. The next time ask them to think of a note – any note to begin with – as they all inhale, and then they should sing that note for as long as their breath lasts. (You could have a competition to see who can hold their note the longest!) They should all stick to their chosen imagined note regardless of what is going on around them!

Then ask them to keep doing this (inhaling and singing a single pitch), but now they can sing different and new pitches on every new breath. Everyone in the group should hold their notes for different durations – some will have stronger breath control than others. This should mean that all the sung pitches overlap, creating an ever-changing chordal context.

In fact, each student should be encouraged to listen to the evolving chordal landscape around them and change their pitches in order to change the chords which emerge from the group. This kaleidoscope of pitches could go on for a long time.

Then ask the students what the music sounded like. What did it remind them of? What was the mood of the music they have just made? Was it scary? Was it relaxing? etc. There is no wrong answer, but it can point the way for them to imagine music being made out of the simplest means.

Then they can go to their instruments. The wind players can operate on the same basis as the singing game. But the other players (strings, keyboards, percussion, guitars etc) can still use the inhale/exhale idea to shape the length of their notes, ie play the note for as long as their breath lasts.

You could use the 'all notes available' format as before OR you could ask them to restrict their pitch choices to the Dorian Mode, starting on the note D.

Example 18

Dorian Mode on D

As they become more confident (singing or playing) you could ask them to shape each note with *crescendo* and *diminuendo*.

Then ask similar questions as before: what does this music sound like? What did it remind them of? What was the mood of the music they have just made? Was it scary? Was it relaxing? etc. There is no wrong answer, but it can point the way for them to imagine music being made out of the simplest means.

Timbre

The language of a note

Sitting in a circle and using voices, pass one pitch around the circle (again middle C or the D above works well for most mixed groups), each person in turn changing its timbre, attack, rhythm, vowel sound, volume, etc before they pass it on to the next person. Make sure each student establishes their own version of the note so that it is properly heard by the rest of the group before the next person begins theirs, but aim to overlap the notes so that there is no silence.

Variations

- Add instruments to the voices.

- Experiment with extended techniques. For string instruments you can suggest *col legno* (tapping the string or bowing the string with the wood of the bow), *sul ponticello* (bowing near the bridge), *sul tasto* (bowing on the fingerboard), *pizzicato* (plucking the string), and *senza* or *molto vibrato* (without, or with exaggerated *vibrato*). For wind players, suggest trying flutter-tonguing or rapid changes of dynamic.

It is always good practice to imagine the type of sound you require when writing music. So if we write a melody for example, we should really try to hear it, or imagine it, on the instrument(s) we are creating it for rather than writing the melody and then thinking, 'I'll put that on a clarinet'. Getting inside the sound is very important for aural training and will result in us making informed decisions about orchestration as our skills progress. If we know about the full range of sounds available from an instrument we have a far greater palette of colours available to us. Knowing what a muted viola sounds like (in every octave), or a cello played near the bridge, should be an integral part of learning about instruments and composition.

- Repeat the 'language of a note' exercise and identify the techniques the students are using. Again, recording an exercise such as this will be a useful reminder during the compositional process.

Try and find recordings which demonstrate the wide variety of timbres and playing techniques available from the instruments within the orchestra; muted trumpets for instance, muted strings en masse, or as a solo, etc. Keep the learning in context. Real composers use these techniques. They are not hard to achieve. The Berio *Sequenzas*, for solo instruments, provide a very clear example of the potential of each instrument. These could be a good place to start. The next two examples are by James MacMillan. The first could be for violin, the second for trumpet, flute or clarinet and both are based on one note but use various different ways of playing. Try playing them yourself or perhaps your instrumental teacher could demonstrate.

Examples 19 & 20: One-note compositional techniques

Pulse and harmony

- Set up a pulse by counting 1, 2, 3, 4, 5, 6, 7, 8.
- Once established, 'feel' it rather than count it aloud. (Keep it in your big toe!)
- Everyone shuts their eyes and claps only on the 1st beat.
- Encourage concentration so that everyone keeps together.

Variations

- Clap on more than one beat ie, the 1st and 7th, again aiming to keep together.

Example 21

- Instead of clapping, add percussion, each group using only one timbre ie, wood, metal, shaker, etc, and add a further number to your pattern.

Example 23

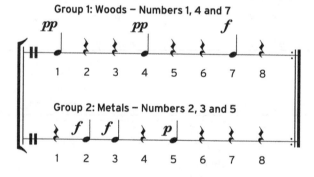

- Set up an irregular pulse ie, 5 or 7.

Example 24

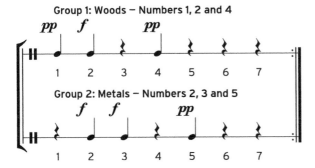

Group 1: Woods – Numbers 1, 2 and 4

Group 2: Metals – Numbers 2, 3 and 5

Starting point for composition

This is a good introduction to irregular meter and also to the role of silence in music. A simple minimalist piece can be created on this basis fairly quickly and very effectively.

If the student chooses a pulse, let's say seven crotchets in the bar, and something is going to happen on 1, 2 and 4, then we have the start of a piece. The subsequent decisions to be made are: what are the events on the 1st, 2nd and 4th beats going to consist of? What instruments will you use and how will they be played? How loud? What pitches? What register? How many times will the pattern repeat?

How could the piece then develop? Through the addition of other instruments and other pitches, we can in turn build harmony. In the next example, all the pitches come from the Dorian mode on D.

Example 25: Dorian mode on D

The flute starts out following the rhythms of the woods then joins the metals, with the addition of quavers and semiquavers so that there is some rhythmic variety between the instruments. The piano follows the metals initially then includes the 1st beat of the bar which belonged to the woods.

What happens if we shift the rhythm one beat forward or back? In this example, the woods and the metals are actually playing the same rhythm, just starting on a different beat of the bar. That rhythm could start on any beat from 1 to 7.

What happens if we add a layer of the same rhythmic pattern in quavers or minims (augmentation or diminution)? The results are all interesting.

We can combine any of the material generated here and we'd have a substantial piece of music. The crucial question when working within a minimalist genre is: how long should a repeated pattern or rhythm continue before something has to change?

Using some of these ideas, see where your students could take this piece. How could they develop it? How could the ideas evolve? Ask them to write another 8 or 16 bars and then play the results. Choose instruments available in the class so that they can hear the results. How fast should it go? Think about the range of dynamics available. Look at articulation. It's the detail that makes a repeating pattern sound interesting and gives it a sense of direction and purpose.

Imagine improvising a set of loops:

1) One is a drone, played by either one instrument or a group of instruments which pass the note around from player to player.

2) Above this a player imagines a two-note phrase. There are lots of decisions to be made about these two notes! Are they high? Are they low? Are they one of each? Are they short? Are they long? Are they one of each? Are they loud or quiet? Or one of each? Once an idea is settled upon, other players can play along with their version of a two-note phrase, played simultaneously, creating a chordal effect.

3) Against this, a player imagines a three-note phrase. There are lots of decisions to be made about these three notes! Are they high? Are they low? Or a mixture of high and low? Are they short? Are they long? Or a mixture of short and long? Loud or quiet, or a mixture? Once an idea is settled upon other players can play along with their version of a three-note phrase, played simultaneously, creating a chordal effect.

4) On top of this a player imagines a four-note phrase, and a similar pattern can begin.

And so we have a piece of music where a number of different loops (based on the numbers one, two, three and four) are rotating in counterpoint. On top of it all a soloist can improvise a fuller, more expansive melody.

Just as the drone is continuous, so the two-note phrases, three-note phrases, four-note phrases and melody on the top also need to be continuous. Each phrase should be followed by a rest and then repeated over and over again, thus creating a rich contrapuntal texture built out of loops (like tape loops). It would also be interesting if the length of each rest was different so that the phrases never really coincide.

It might also be interesting at some stage to drop the drone completely, leaving the music more sparse. If and when the drone is re-introduced it could be on a different pitch.

Harmony and rhythm

Decide how many beats you want in the bar. For the purpose of this exercise, any number between 4 and 10 would work well. Split the class into three or four groups. Each group then chooses two beats of the bar on which they would like an event to happen ie, if the bar is to have 7 beats they could choose beats 3 and 7, or beats 2 and 5. Each group then goes on to create two chords based on pitches from the Dorian mode (or pentatonic scale, or any other series). Groups can then set up a pulse and perform their chords for the class, playing on their chosen beats for a crotchet only. Once every group has performed their chords separately, try performing the chords from two or more groups together. Listen out for the shifts in harmony.

Example 26

Group 1: Beats 3 and 7

Group 2: Beats 2 and 5

Now sustain the chords and move to the next one on the correct beat. Again, listen to the harmony created with the other group.

Example 27

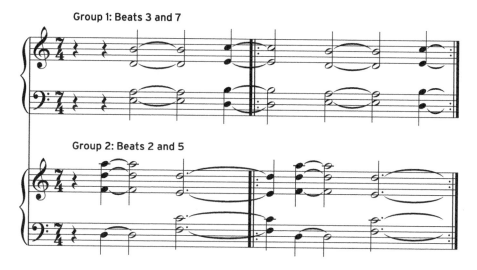

Starting point for composition

This kind of slowly shifting harmony can be extremely effective. When the pitches overlap in different ways and for different lengths of time, the harmony can change through time. Decide how many repetitions of this one bar you want to hear, then change to a new and different version using different beats of the bar and different pitches. How many overlapping chords can we use before the texture becomes muddy? Helmut Lachenmann, in No. 5 from *Kinderspiel* (seven short pieces for piano), uses overlapping chords as the principal for the whole piece. This is a good exercise for piano or keyboard players and could be a useful piece to look at with your students.

All of these games and exercises can be extended as appropriate for the class and modified for most age groups. Games are a way of creating musical material spontaneously. They give young composers the chance to try out techniques as a class before they embark on longer pieces on their own. They also provide an opportunity to be constructively critical of each other's work. Again, it is important to stress that there is no 'right and wrong' in composition, rather 'more or less effective'. It is the level of effectiveness that we should look at when we are being critical of a piece, and that will often depend on what the child has managed to communicate through their work. Many of these exercises can also be used as a fun and spontaneous introduction to the compositional process. Music making can and indeed, should always, retain its element of fun!

4 Composition – a decision-making process

Worksheet for use in the classroom (photocopyable); description of process and all decisions

A step-by-step guide to the compositional process

When you start teaching composition, you have to look really hard at your own compositional processes so that you can begin to guide the next generation in the most effective way possible. Everyone is different and every composer works in a different way, but there are some useful generalities that can help all of us as we start a new piece.

Pre-compositional work is of an equal, if not greater, importance than the actual writing down of ideas, and when you identify what needs to be done and in what order, it becomes possible to extract a process which very much helps both in the teaching of the craft and in the writing of the piece. It is the series of decisions that you make about every aspect of the process that ultimately provides a road map that can help.

Through participation in some of the games and exercises in the previous chapter, young composers will now be able to see that there is no mystery to this thing called composition. It is a myth of course that composers sit and wait for the muse to hit them and that when it does, they go off into their shed and beaver away until the work is done. This is not the case at all, and if we did wait for the muse, we would be waiting forever!! The learning of a sound technique, and ways to overcome the inevitable writers' block are what we need to address with young composers. Decision-making itself is not always easy, but it certainly beats staring at a blank page wondering how on earth you're going to fill it up!

The following worksheet for students is followed by explanatory notes for teachers and will take you through the whole decision-making process so that each young composer has the opportunity to create something unique that expresses something of themselves.

The following worksheet is available to download here:
trinitycollege.com/music-books

Composition – the decision-making process

Composing music is all about making decisions. Our decisions will be rooted in why we are writing each piece and what we want to say through our music. Some of the decisions we have to make are:

1. What is my piece going to be about (if anything)?
Do I want to try to communicate an idea, a place, a feeling, an event, or will it be entirely abstract?

2. Title
Once you have decided what you want to write about, give it a title. This will focus your energies in one direction and will remind you what, exactly, you are intending to communicate.

3. Instrumentation
What instruments am I going to include in my piece?

4. Structure and length
How long will my piece be when it is complete? Will it be in one long section or in two or three or more? Will any of the sections repeat? Will the speed change when I start a new section? How long will the sections be?

5. Speed
How fast will the music go?

6. Pitch
When you begin writing your piece you will have to make decisions about what pitches you want to use. You could limit your pitches to one scale or a mode, or another collection or series. You could use tonal harmony, or experiment with atonal sounds.

7. Key signature
Will my piece be in a certain key or will I use accidentals where appropriate?

8. Rhythm
Experiment with rhythms. Again, you will have to make decisions about whether you want to use rhythms which are similar or they could be totally different from one another. Think about layering rhythms.

9. Time signature
Does my piece need a time signature? Will the time signature change at some point during the piece?

Note: *Every decision you make should help you communicate your original intention through your music.*

5 What do you want to write about?

What you want to say and why; how to interrogate your idea; ideas that will help us or hinder us; further study – The Confession of Isobel Gowdie

The decision as to what the student is going to write about will inform all of their subsequent decisions, so don't move on until they are absolutely convinced that they've hit on something that is going to interest them and keep them interested. Any idea, no matter how abstract, can be translated into music in some way. Often the initial idea will inform the whole structure of the piece. If they decide to communicate an event from history for example, encourage the pupil to think around that subject so that they can begin to picture it as fully as possible in their mind.

The teacher could ask the following questions:

- What sort of event was this? Describe it to me.
- Was it a sad or happy event?
- Was the event turbulent or serene?
- Anything else you can remember?
- Why is this event important to you?

So, to turn this idea into a piece of music, we need to identify the ideas that are most important and most useful to us as composers.

For example, what does the student want to convey about what happened? How might they do that? There are obviously several ways, which could employ a variety of musical devices appropriate to the level of musicianship. For instance, try a repetitive ostinato: rhythmic, melodic or harmonic. This could provide a background layer of sound that goes on and on. Or what about a very quiet sound, gently repeating, as if it were in the distance. It could get nearer and therefore louder as the piece progressed or vice versa.

What about the feelings evoked by what happened? Were the events happy or sad? You might want to start thinking about happy sounding harmonies, instrumental combinations or rhythms, or the sad equivalents.

The student could map out the potential shape of the piece in advance. A graph could be made of what he/she wants the music to do, where it should go, and what its main characteristics might be. For example, in James MacMillan's *The Confession of Isobel Gowdie* the opening section is serene and prayerful and there is no hint of the violence to come. The middle section implies some of the frightening things about Isobel's confession and demise. The final section brings back the serenity from the opening although it has been affected and changed by the intervening convulsions. We might map the entire work in three parts then:

Fig. 1: Map of *Confession of Isobel Gowdie*

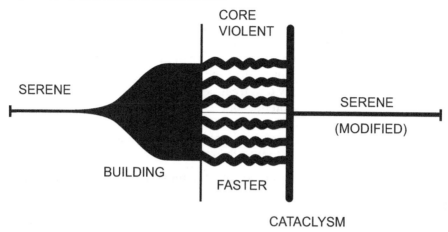

Once the student has decided on the great idea for the piece, encourage them to find a title for it. It will help focus their energies and remind them of what they are trying to achieve every time they go back to working on it. Titles can offer a sense of the mood of the music or can be more whimsical. It really doesn't matter which, but a composer must be able to reasonably justify their decision.

It could be useful to see how James MacMillan might interrogate an idea for a new piece, in this case, his orchestral work *The Confession of Isobel Gowdie*. In the 'Further Study' (overleaf) he describes how he could see potential in Isobel Gowdie's story, then explains some of the research and thinking he undertook and finally, how he translated his response to the ideas in to musical material.

Further study:

The Confession of Isobel Gowdie – James MacMillan

I discovered the story of Isobel Gowdie on reading *The History of the Scottish People* by Scottish historian T.C. Smout. Although there may be some conjecture about the facts and significance of her life and death, it is clear that she was a real person who lived near Nairn in the 17th century. She has been the object of some fascination over the years from writers, musicians and dramatists. Looking back on my own treatment of her story, I do remember being struck at the dramatic potential of the tale, first and foremost. In fact, my first instinct was to imagine one possible treatment of the story as an opera, and I still think it would make a very exciting opera. Until only very recently, I imagined I would return to it in that form in the future.

Nevertheless, because the story is so vivid the music of the orchestral tone poem could not help but be shaped and guided by some sense of narrative. This gave me cause for some reflection at the time. Why? Principally, because the orchestral tone poem, in all its picture-painting, story-telling implications is a Romantic, 19th century phenomenon, and it would surely be seen as odd that the form could be resurrected at the end of the 20th century. Could it be done? And why would any 'modern' composer want to do it?

In 1662 Isobel Gowdie from Nairn confessed to having been baptised by the devil and joining a coven of 13 who met at night; she had journeyed to the centre of the earth to feast with the King and Queen of the fairies; she could fly, or become a hare, a cat or a crow; she used waxen images and bags of boiled toads to cause inflictions; she had killed a ploughman with elf-arrows the devil gave her.

Initially I was drawn by the dramatic and programmatic potential of this terrible story but the work soon developed a far more emotional core as I attempted to draw together various strands in a single, complicated act of contrition. Rather grandiosely at the time, I imagined that, on behalf of the Scottish people, the work craved absolution and offered Isobel Gowdie the mercy and humanity that was denied her in the last days of her life. To do this I tried to capture the soul of Scotland in music, and the outer sections contain a multitude of chants, songs and litanies (real and imagined) coming together in a reflective outpouring – a prayer for the murdered woman.

So this act of solidarity, if you like, which is described here, or this retrospective act of compassion which is implied in the motivation for taking the work beyond the Romantic tone poem, to make it something else – what could that actually mean in purely musical terms? What would 'the soul of Scotland in music' actually mean in concrete abstract terms?

Well there needed to be some real Scottish musical heritage invoked here or alluded to, to point in this particular direction. And therefore the modality of the music is deliberate, as is the ornamentation, and the keening, bending, almost vocal lamenting sounds in the string counterpoint at the beginning.

In the years prior to the composition of *Confession* I had immersed myself in Scottish and Irish folk music, joining a few bands as a whistle player, keyboardist and singer, performing around the folk clubs and pubs in the west of Scotland. I got to know traditional singers like Heather Heywood, and worked with them, but more importantly I listened carefully to them sing, and became aware of the deep reservoir of songs that they had on tap, and of their performance techniques. I also listened attentively, especially to the pipers and fiddlers I worked with. I believe that this was the central experience which shaped the mood and emotion of the outer sections in the *Confession*.

Of interest might be the opening on clarinets and bassoons, where there is an oscillation of principal pitches outlining the mode, which soon gives way to the strings. Of central importance here are the violas and cellos – in rehearsal they always notice how much more difficult their music is compared to the violins and basses! In vocal terms you could imagine their music being 'led' by expressive tenors – such as in Gaelic Psalm singing where the Cantor leads the assembly which follow him in a shady, heterophonous, imitative unity.

The entry at the end of bar 25 in the 2nd basses is important – it is a quotation from the 'Lux Aeterna' of the *Requiem Mass*. (Let perpetual light shine upon her.) It is quoted deliberately to focus the musical and extra-musical purpose and direction of the piece. The remainder of this section remains settled in the now-established mode: C D E F♯ G A B. This changes at letter D with the introduction of F and B♭ – foreign notes – but the first in outlining another melodic/harmonic field. This linking passage (up to letter E) is more complex tonally as the trumpet heterophony is underpinned by very rich and dark chords, pointing forward to the violence to come.

The music from letter E can be analysed according to the layers of material which make up the complexity here: a) the trombones and tuba have the 'Lux Aeterna' theme, this time harmonised as a chorale, b) the horns are like hunting horns – full of open-air, brash and extrovert braying, with lots of ornamental flurries, c) the drummers face each other across the orchestra, sometimes sharing in a two note 'heartbeat' but then going on to a hocketting 'conversation' based on that rhythm, d) a harmonic field appears in the upper strings and upper woodwind which creates a cloud effect – something ethereal floating above everything else, e) underneath an ominous rumbling and surging starts growing in the cellos and basses.

The B♭/F music returns with the trumpets at letter G, but by this stage the onward momentum from the lower instruments is underway and pushing towards even greater turbulence. The climax of all this is the violent, full *tutti* repetition of 13 strokes! (Isobel Gowdie confessed to being part of a coven of 13 witches.) This is the beginning of the Development section where a number of these elements are now in battle with each other. The music goes through a series of metric modulations, but when these occur there are always two of the main oppositional 'themes' at loggerheads with each other. One is the 13 strokes, representative of the powers of evil perhaps (see bar 154 onwards), and the other is the 'Lux Aeterna' theme, representative of the elemental opposite, the force of goodness and grace. We see this clash again at bar 181 onwards, and then again at bar 209 onwards etc. The metric modulation obviously cranks up the tempo of the music which now becomes faster and faster.

When it can become no faster and no more violent, it gives way unexpectedly to the 'Lux Aeterna' theme again in lower strings, very quietly and slowly at bar 345. This interaction between utmost violence and serene but brooding tranquillity continues, and constitutes the climax of the work through to letter V, where a recapitulation of the opening string threnody is finally established. This repeat from here is mostly literal, but perhaps feels different because of what the intervening musical journey has involved.

6 Instrumentation

Timbre; combining sounds; musical intention

When you bake a chocolate sponge, you ensure that the ingredients are the most appropriate available to you, ie, those which will enable you to create the best chocolate sponge possible. You would not start adding potatoes or vinegar to the sponge because you would be creating something other than a chocolate sponge if you did. Similarly in music, the ingredients, or instruments you choose to write for, will be defined by what you are trying to say, achieve and create. If the idea is that you will write a lullaby, you are unlikely to decide to write for trombones, tubas and bagpipes. Encourage each pupil to imagine the type of sound they hear in their head for the opening notes of their piece. What is the combination they want their audience to hear first? Encourage them to learn about the capabilities of each instrument they have selected. It is not good enough to know the lowest and highest note when the 'sounds' of each register are so distinct, for example. Instrumentation is too often left to chance or defined by what is available in the class. Through careful listening to some recorded excerpts, young composers can hear what can be achieved with only one instrument.

If a young composer plays an instrument themselves, that is always a good place to start. Pointing out the different colours of sounds available, the timbres, the textures in music they are learning, can also inspire a story for a new piece. Inspiration can come from anywhere. Defining what you want to write about can emerge from analytical listening, to your own playing or to recordings of solo or ensemble works.

For example:

James MacMillan, *After the Tryst*

Britten, *Metamorphosen after Ovid* for Solo Oboe

J.S. Bach, *Partitas* for Solo Violin

J. S. Bach, *Suites* for Solo Cello

Lachenmann, *Kinderspiel* for Solo Piano

Berio, *Sequenza IX* for Clarinet, *Sequenza XII* for Bassoon

Britten, *The Young Person's Guide to the Orchestra*
This is an orchestral piece but it allows the composer to hear each orchestral instrument one after the other in a way that can be extremely useful.

A young composer doesn't need to use a lot of instruments to provide contrast if they know the full capability of those they have selected.

Word of warning: all too often young composers work out their compositions on electronic keyboards. These have a wealth of sounds which are undoubtedly interesting to experiment with, but many are unreal or synthesised. When a student decides to write for the 'tubular bell' sound for instance, do they think about the pitch range available on the instrument or what type of hammers the percussionist will need for the desired affect? Or are they writing for 'tubular bell sound' on a particular keyboard which can achieve a particular volume depending on how high the volume knob is turned up?

This practice means the composer will need to know nothing more than the number to punch into the keyboard for 'tubular bells' or 'string sounds'. They would then write a piece for these instruments as they would write a keyboard piece but learn nothing of the component parts of a 'string sound' or the register or range of tubular bells. This is definitely something worth thinking about and raising with young composers who work in this way, even if only to alert them to the problems they would encounter in a live performance of what they have written.

It is also commonplace now for young composers to write their music with the help of music notation software, and the same issues arise. Unless you have an amazing sound card in your computer, you will miss a great deal of the subtleties of live instruments. Your ear is not exercised in the same way as it would be if you sit with your paper and pencil, crafting each individual note and rhythm. You don't become as immersed in your material and you really don't develop your inner ear in the way you could. By all means typeset a completed piece with any software available, but don't be tempted to compose directly on to the computer.

7 Structure and length

*The washing line; defining the structure; formal structures
that are useful; breaking your own rules*

You might be surprised to find that it would not be unusual for a composer to know exactly how long their piece was going to be before they had even written a note. This could be in terms of the number of beats or bars, or more likely, the number of seconds. For young composers, the idea of telling them to write a piece that lasts 145 seconds would be ridiculous, but again, through analysis, we can see that a number of the movements in the Suites of Bach for instance, consist of two halves of the same number of bars (8, 10, 12), both repeated. This is a structure, and it can be very useful to us. Composition is a difficult enough process so anything that makes it easier should be encouraged!

If you want to tell a friend about a storm you got caught up in when you were on holiday last month, your story could last anything from one sentence to an hour-long ramble! The same is true if you wanted to express your storm in music. You have to consider how much detail you want to impart to your audience and think about how long your audience will want (or be able) to maintain their interest. Chances are that the telling of your story will be much more effective if you keep it concise rather than starting at the beginning and finishing when you run out of steam (or when your audience has got up and left or fallen asleep!). If you are writing a melody, decide that it will last four bars, or five bars, (or however many number of bars) before you begin. Since you know where you are heading, perhaps by deciding to modulate in these four or five bars, (or not!), or you know that you want to end on a long tonic, it will be far easier to get there. If you know where you are going when you leave the house in the morning, you have a far better chance of arriving where you want to be!

Everything that changes through time has its own structure. Walking along the road is a structured activity. Two objects, the feet, hit the pavement alternately and propel the body through the environment. A burning candle has a structure. The wick burns down, making the wax melt, which in turn drips down the side of the candle. This transforms the original shape of the candle into a new form. The flame flickers and is then still again. All this happens through time and can be analysed or defined in terms of a structure.

We have been extremely lucky in our careers to have had access to some wonderful composition teachers, all of whom passed on nuggets of wisdom that remain extremely useful. One of the most valuable descriptions of structure we inherited, which we now pass on to all of our school students at some time or other, is that of the bending ruler.

Imagine holding a plastic ruler at each end, bending it and bending it, increasing the tension, changing the shape, but not the intrinsic 'rulerness' of the ruler. After some time (how much time?!) it breaks into tiny pieces which are scattered everywhere and you are left with two larger bits of ruler, one in each hand. Something has happened to the ruler through time. It has been transformed from a relaxed item, through a process of increasing tension, to a defined point when the tension got so great that it snapped. It was turned into two big bits and lots of scattered little bits. That process could then become a musical structure as something has changed over time. We could draw this transformation as follows.

Fig. 2: Bending the ruler

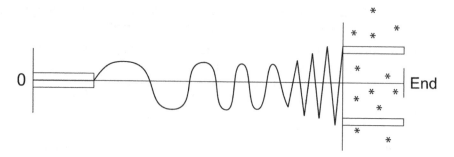

We have started with a solid piece of plastic, which exists for its own sake: ie, we have started with a ruler. The ruler then experiences an increase in tension across its entire length because it is being bent from each end. That tension becomes greater and greater before the ruler breaks in two with shards spinning off in all directions. So, how does this structure have anything to do with music? What does solid sound like in music? What sounds, pitches or rhythms could exist for their own sake? What happens to this sound when tension is added? Does it become faster, louder? How do we create tension in music? Then at the point when the ruler breaks in two, what could that mean for our musical material? How do small fragments of music go off in all directions? What does that mean for our pitch, rhythm, register, pace, etc? The above timeline then becomes a map not only of ruler breaking but also of a musical process.

Suggest to each pupil that they produce some sort of timeline or map for their piece. Once decisions are made as to what the work is to be about and what the music needs to communicate, then thinking about sections, the development of ideas and how the piece will grow as time passes is always helpful. Shapes and contours of dynamic ranges can be added, and textures drawn in, the end result being an overall sketch of the intention of the music.

This is of course before we have even thought about a single pitch, harmony or rhythm. Defining how our material will function in hypothetical terms gives us a better chance of achieving our aims when the actual musical material is added. Again, if you know where you are going when you leave the house in the morning, you have a far better chance of arriving where you want to be! Here are a few examples of timelines:

Fig. 3: The gradual *crescendo*

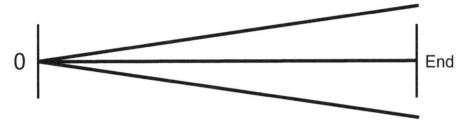

Fig. 4: A walk along the Brora Beach

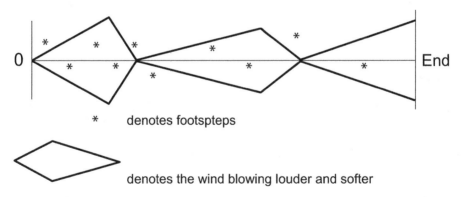

*   denotes footspteps

denotes the wind blowing louder and softer

Fig. 5: A burning candle

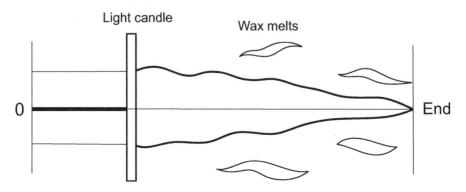

Having a plan in front of us is a compositional aid, not a prescription for our piece. As the composer, we have the ultimate right to change the shape of our piece as we go on, but if we have a map to follow we are more likely to make logical and sensible changes rather than spur of the moment ones derived from problems in controlling our musical material.

We cannot stress enough the value in pre-compositional planning in this way. It may seem that the process is becoming somewhat mechanical, but you will find that the more parameters the young composer can control, the easier it will be to write the piece.

Try this exercise with your class:
Write eight bars of spooky music on one note for one instrument. When you take away the vast number of instruments and pitches that are available to us, we need only think of how best to express our aim. How do we express 'spooky' on a high cello D note? We have to think very hard about the type of sound we want, what playing technique will let us achieve that, what dynamic will we start on, the rhythm of our single pitch, etc.

If we help a young composer create boundaries within which to work, then the task is so much more specific and achievable. The blank page is all too daunting.

Speed

How fast or how slow the music will go is again defined by what the composer is writing about and what they are trying to achieve. A simple Italian term is fine, or a metronome marking with a couple of words to clarify the mood is good too, and vital for an accurate performance of the music.

For example: ♩ = 114 **Perky, joyful**

We may think we know how fast we want it to go but we must communicate that in our score and parts. Similarly, tempo changes within a piece should be carefully considered. Will the music get faster towards a section change or slower towards the end? We might need to alter the tempo marking, or an *accelerando* or *rallentando* or similar might be enough to express what we want.

8 Pitch

*Freedom in limitation; scales and modes; harmony;
melody; motivic development*

By this stage, each pupil will have a clear idea of what their piece is to be about. They will have a detailed structural plan or timeline, know what instruments they are writing for and the speed of the opening, but they haven't yet written a note. How do we make decisions as to what pitches we are going to use and what informs these decisions? Again, the answer should be linked directly to what the work is to communicate and to some extent, which instruments the composer has selected.

If you pare down the number of pitches before you begin, chances are you will achieve your intention more succinctly than ambling away, just going with what sounds nice. Young composers often find the starting point for their pieces by working at the keyboard, so when they come up with a phrase that sounds appropriate, analyse the content (the intervals, the repeated pitches, why it sounds nice), and use these ideas to develop it on the page rather than carrying on at the keyboard.

Encourage your pupils to define a group of pitches or series, or a mode or scale, within which they are going to work. This is particularly valuable for those who find 'getting started' the biggest hurdle. Often if we have too many things to choose from we will make a less informed choice about what is better and what could be discarded. If you pare down the variety of pitches that you can use, then your compositional decisions will be rooted in technique and intention to communicate.

Starting point for composition

Suggest a mood to the class, for example, 'scary'. Limit the pitches they are allowed to use to the traditional pentatonic scale (black notes on the piano) and ask them to write eight bars of the scariest music possible for piano.

Variations

- Suggest each pupil selects their own combination of five pitches and write in another mood for their own instrument and piano.
- Add one further pitch halfway through the piece. What happens to the tonality or harmony?

There are many existing scales or modes that the class could use as a starting point and of course, the familiar major or minor scales and the Blues scale.

Example 28: Scales and Modes
A downloadable version can be found here: **trinitycollege.com/music-books**

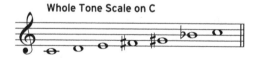

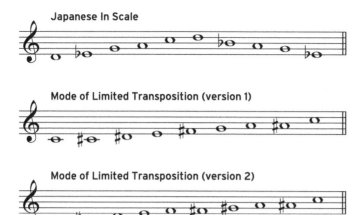

Combining scales often gives rise to new and interesting harmonic possibilities. If you use a pentatonic scale (the black notes on the piano) and a Dorian mode on D together, you can create all sorts of unusual harmonies.

Once each composer has found the pitches they want to work with on a keyboard, always suggest they move away and write out combinations of pitches and chords on paper. They can then go back to the keyboard to try out what they have come up with and listen to the sounds they have created. Our hands so often fall onto the keys in familiar shapes that, chances are, we will miss combinations of sounds that might be interesting because our fingers don't find them. Always encourage the class to work both ways, from the keyboard (or their own instrument) onto paper and from the paper onto their instrument.

Key signatures

If you are writing in a specific tonal area then it helps a performer if a key signature is present. Similarly, if there is ambiguity as to the tonal centre then accidentals, where appropriate, are all that is required.

If we decide to work in a particular key, then look at ways of moving through related keys as the music progresses. The traditionally related keys – dominant, subdominant, relative major or minor, tonic major or minor – are always a safe bet, but further up the curriculum you might want to move further afield. As we know, modulation to any key is perfectly achievable and, if managed carefully, can be extremely effective.

9 Rhythm

Freedom in limitation; repetition; rate of harmonic change; time signatures

Rhythm is a concept often intrinsically related to melody or harmony; melody has its own rhythm and the rate of change of harmony provides another rhythm. The composer may decide however, that rhythm should be the prime concept for a piece – the concept which underpins the music totally. So we could decide to write a piece for untuned percussion only, where rhythm will be central to the development of the whole piece as seen earlier in Chapter 3.

Rhythm can also be used as a device for quickening pace, or adding a cultural idiosyncrasy to a work (the scotch snap for instance). Climax can be achieved by speeding up the rate of change of harmony, and augmentation and diminution can apply to rhythm, melody and harmonic change.

Do encourage experimentation with accents and the number of beats in the bar. Using $\frac{5}{4}$ or $\frac{7}{8}$ time signatures is not as difficult as it might seem.

Time signatures and barlines are tools to help make sense of the music and subsequently the reading and performing of the piece. If the time signature needs to change, then change it. Keep things simple, but do experiment with the effects of changing accents in a bar. There is added interest in the momentum of the music if there is an occasional bar with an unexpected accent or an uneven number of beats in it. Look again at some of the games and exercises in Chapter 3. These will give you all sorts of ideas to suggest to your own pupils.

Now that the crucial decisions have been made we are ready to start writing the piece. The plan of the structure has been developed, the instrumentation has been decided upon, we know what shape the piece will take, and the pitches and harmony have been selected. The process should now have its own momentum and the piece should almost write itself... almost!

Encourage the class to document and justify their decisions as they go. If a pupil cannot justify a decision then the chances are it will be because it hasn't been considered in the light of communicating the initial thought or idea. Always question decisions and seek justification. If a pupil has an understanding of how they have arrived at the piece they are writing, they will have full ownership of the process from beginning to end. This is vital if they are to remain interested enough to complete the task in hand. They will also have a better chance of being able to repeat the process for the next and subsequent pieces. This is the start of learning a compositional technique.

---

10 Further techniques, hints and tips

Making the most of your ideas; avoiding idea-overload;
playing around with material; writing it all down

A useful piece of advice for all composers is: **don't cram too many ideas into one piece; rather, use what you have in new and different ways.**

It is a good idea to start exploring the potential of even the tiniest bit of material from the earliest stages of learning compositional technique. If we use the process of analysis, of the great composers for example as a way into that exploration, the pupils' learning will be put into context, and that is really what we are aiming for.

For instance: look at what Beethoven did with his four-note fragment in the 5th Symphony. How did he use its rhythmic properties, melodic properties, timbral properties? How did it expand as the work progressed? Try to access the score of the piece you're discussing with your class, so that they can see clearly what the motif looks like on the page, how it evolves, how it is repeated, how it develops.

There are some brilliant resources available online now where you can hear a piece being performed as the score is seen on the screen.

Developing melody

James MacMillan on *After the Tryst*

Melodic lines are as important in modern composition as in any previous time. Some like to joke that modern composers 'don't write tunes any more!' This is wrong. Perhaps the 'tunes' are stranger than one might expect from earlier music but the importance of the 'single line' is still central to a composer's thinking.

Luciano Berio wrote a series of *Sequenzas* for solo instruments (including voice) which are revolutionary, inventive and worth a close look. Olivier Messiaen was obsessed with 'monody' and one can find this focus on a melodic core in his organ music and in his instrumental scores. His love of Gregorian chant and plainsong was the motivation here. Many composers have drawn on folk music, which is essentially a melodic phenomenon.

When I was younger I used to play and sing a lot of Scottish and Irish folk music. I set a poem by William Soutar, *The Tryst*, in a style that was meant to sound like an ancient Scottish ballad:

Example 29: Tryst tune

This melody in turn became the basis for further developments. Here is one way of expanding, stretching and varying the material. In this violin piece, *After The Tryst*, you can trace how I used this original melody.

The notes of the original are ringed – but what is happening in between? Sometimes there are 'foreign' chromatic pitches that we would not normally encounter in D major (which is the key of the original tune), such as in bar 2. Sometimes the violin part leaps into higher octaves (bars 4-5).

Sometimes the original notes are held and stretched (bar 5), sometimes there are slides (*glissandi*) between pitches (bar 5), sometimes little two-note fragments are repeated obsessively and violently (bars 7-9), sometimes the music just gets a little bit crazy and virtuosic in a show-off-ish kind of way! (bars 10, 11).

After the Tryst

James MacMillan

The point is that an original melody can be used as 'scaffolding' on which to hang your subsequent melodic variation and development — the original notes can act as a kind of framework for very free invention.

1) Space out the notes of your simple melody on a large piece of manuscript.

2) Now fill in the gaps — be as unusual and eccentric as you want.

If this is too formulaic, just try to take your original melody for a 'walk' and find new ways of linking pitch to pitch as you work through the original material.

Look at as many examples as possible with the scores, in all musical genres, and then listen to them. You will find that the techniques these great composers use are not out of reach of secondary pupils.

A tiny fragment has shape, rhythm, timbre and dynamic, all of which can be developed either independently or together. If we look at the shape of a phrase and examine the full potential of its intervals, we can generate a substantial amount of related material.

Example 30: A simple phrase:

Within this phrase are the intervals of a major 3rd, perfect 5th, minor 2nd and minor 6th. If we simplify its shape diagrammatically:

Fig. 6: A simple phrase as a diagram

If we play around with that shape we could create:

Fig. 7: Upside down (inversion)

If we took it a step further and made it upside-down with repetition of the second peak, and then extend it down more a bit we would come up with something like this:

Fig. 8: Inversion extended through repetition

In notational form we can come up with the following:

Example 31: Upside down (inversion) as notation

Or with the extension (and up an octave):

Example 32: Inversion extended (and up an octave) as notation

If we now analyse the rhythmic structure of the original cell, we can apply all sorts of modifications and again, arrive at quantities of related material.

Example 33: Rhythmic variations of the original idea

Of course, it is the composer's task to select and reject whatever they wish, but by working on the paper in this way you are bound to arrive at fragments you would never have come up with at the keyboard. Doodling with the diagrammatic shapes and then adding pitches from your chosen scale or series that match the contours is also a great way of generating material you might not otherwise find 'under the hands'.

Now, let's look at a tonal chord and analyse its intervallic structure.

Example 34: C major chord

Here we have a major 3rd, a minor 3rd and a perfect 4th, one on top of the other. If we build a chord using the same intervals on each pitch of the first chord (C, E and G), we have two new chords:

Example 35: Major chords built on the pitches of the C major chord

If we then combine the pitches we have arrived at, there are numerous further chords available to us. For example:

Example 36

We can apply similar techniques to atonal chords and arrive at several interesting and related 'pitch fields'. This next chord consists of a major 3rd, a major 3rd and a perfect 5th, one of top of each other. The pitches are C, E, G♯ and D♯. If we create the same relation of a major 3rd, a major 3rd and a perfect 5th on top of each of C, E, G♯ and D♯, we get a series of transpositions of the original chord...

Example 37

Original

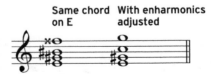

Same chord on E   With enharmonics adjusted

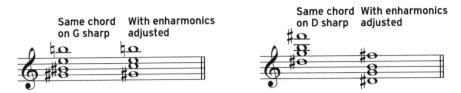

Same chord on G sharp — With enharmonics adjusted

Same chord on D sharp — With enharmonics adjusted

...which we could layer in various combinations.

Example 38

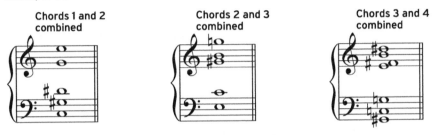

Chords 1 and 2 combined

Chords 2 and 3 combined

Chords 3 and 4 combined

To make sense of the term 'pitch fields', we can relate the idea to our understanding of modulation in tonality. If we start off in a particular key, our material will be rooted in that tonality. When we modulate to the dominant we become rooted in another, related tonality. Similarly if we begin in an atonal field and move to another related field, the function of the move is exactly the same. So the move from one field to another in atonal music is similar to modulation in tonality. As composers, we can define our fields and move freely between them. This movement can be part of the defined structure of the work as a whole. The opening section might use this field:

Example 39: Field 1

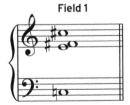

Field 1

After 16 bars we might start a new section in Field 2 (the same chord built on E):

Example 40: Field 2

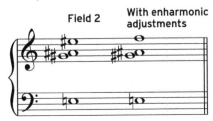

Field 2 — With enharmonic adjustments

Then after another 16 bars we might combine the first two fields to create Field 3:

Example 41: Field 3

Another way of developing a harmonic progression is by using a stock phrase and modifying each chord in some way.

For instance, VI-IIb-V-Ib in C major uses the following pitches:

Example 42: VI-IIb-V-Ib in C major

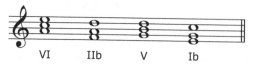

What would happen if we added a further, arbitrary pitch to each of these chords?

Example 43: VI-IIb-V-Ib in C major with added pitches

We arrive at a new progression with a solid bass line but with added interest in the upper parts. Again, try this on paper before taking it to the keyboard to play the results. You will come up with far more unusual combinations of pitches working this way round.

We can also derive rhythm from the intervallic structure of a chord so that all of the musical material we use in a piece is intrinsically related. If we analyse the intervals of a major chord in terms of the number of semitones:

Example 44: Intervals in a C major chord

Four semitones between middle C and E; three semitones between E and G, five semitones between G and top C, we arrive at a series of numbers, four, three, five which can in turn be used as note lengths or number of beats per bar:

Example 45: Semitones of a major chord expressed as note lengths and time signatures

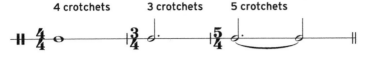

or

Example 46

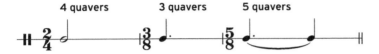

or the number of crotchets between rests:

Example 47: Semitones of a major chord expressed as the number of crotchets between rests

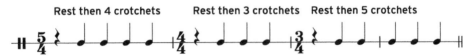

All of these ideas can be further modified through the use of augmentation, diminution, layering, overlapping, etc.

Some of the concepts we are dealing with here are quite complex but still allow for a great deal of flexibility and self-expression. Pitch analysis of 20th century art music is often virtually impossible because of the methods composers use to generate their material. Perhaps by exploring some of the techniques I have described, the class will come up with many more methods of their own.

As a point of reassurance: methodical working like this is absolutely no substitute for intuition and inventiveness. It is all very well generating lots of scrunchy chords, but what exactly are you going to do with them? A composer will need every ounce of their creativity to make sense of them. But at least no-one will be staring at a blank page.

The crucial issue of notation

We write our music down so that it can be played by someone other than ourselves and so that we have some record of our work. If pianist X was to play my brand new 'Piano Piece', we could probably assume that pianist X had never played any of my music before and that they had never heard my 'Piano Piece' played by anyone else. Therefore the music that I give them must include all the information they will require to enable them to perform my intentions accurately.

Traditional staff notation is, of course, the most widely used in the western classical tradition. All of our orchestral musicians learn it and use it throughout their careers. We learn it as we learn to play our instruments at school or sing in a choir. We have to remember though, that in other parts of the world, the aural tradition might be the predominant way of learning music, or notation might be completely different to our own. If we look at how music for the gamelan is notated, or for the Japanese shakuhachi, we begin to realise that there are many ways in which musical intention can be expressed.

We would stress again however, the value in the teaching of traditional staff notation. It provides us, in the vast majority of circumstances, with the symbols or words that we require to convey our ideas accurately. Contemporary composers do find however that they have to invent new ways of expressing something very specific and we shouldn't be afraid to do this as and when the need arises. If we include a detailed explanation of what we mean in the introduction to the piece, then we can expect a player to execute exactly what we require.

Graphic notations have their use in works which have elements of aleatoricism, or are semi-improvised. We must never use this method as a get-out of detailing exactly what we want however. If we leave too much to the discretion of the performer, we have to wonder who has actually written the piece.

If we examine some of the notation of Trevor Wishart for example in his *Vox Cycle*, or that of Xenakis in his percussion piece, *Psappha*, we can see the level of complexity they have achieved. There are disadvantages to this type of notating however; performers don't only have to learn the notes, they are having to learn a completely new language of symbols or boxes. These are not pieces that many people will ever manage to perform.

There are no easy answers to writing music down if there is no prior knowledge of traditional notation. The only solution would be to devise what is needed as the piece progresses. Shapes, colours and textures can all come in handy, but always include a detailed explanation in the score.

11 Conclusion

1) **Be bold in your teaching**
   Teaching composition to teenagers is a perfect opportunity for the class to broaden its musical horizons, even in the type of music that is being listened to by the individuals involved. Sticking to what is known already, or to a few sanctioned templates in the curriculum could lead to a restriction of musical vision, ambition and options. The composition courses taught in schools allow the class to explore the unknown. It may be that this leads to discoveries of older classical music, or more modern classical music, but it could also open doorways to music from different cultures or less obvious popular musics.

   What about Indian ragas? Or Javanese gamelan? Or Mongolian Tuvan throat singing? Or big band music from the 1950s? Or folk music from Scandinavia? The world of music can open up, and all these unexpected discoveries can lead the way to untold and unexplored avenues in the students' compositional imaginations too.

2) **Don't be afraid of experimenting with new compositional techniques as you support the next generation**
   Moving attention sideways from what might be expected could be the key here to unlocking the imagination. What if you don't start with a melody for example? What if you thought of some other parameter as the starting point? Some other musical feature as the priority instead of a 'tune', for example? What if the focus was specifically and pointedly on harmony, or a series of chords? Floating chords (unrelated to a controlling melody) can be very evocative and atmospheric. They can create new colours and surprising moods. Be bold in the make-up of the chords. They don't need to be major or minor. They can contain lots of pitches – and experimenting with interval types in these chords could be revelatory.

   Or what if rhythm was the prime focus and not harmony or melody? What would the music be like if the student (or students) were to begin by pounding out repeated pulses, notes or chords like that famous moment in Stravinsky's *Rite of Spring*? Or what if you used numbers to make a series of pitches? It doesn't need to be a 12-note series: it could be a smaller number that is associated with a mode, for example.

3) **Don't get tied up in the issues of assessment – they restrict creativity and experimentation**
   If the student or the teacher gets curtailed by box-ticking to suit the curriculum it could impact negatively on the imagination. Composing new

music should be an exciting step into the unknown. Yes, I'm sure some of it will, and should perhaps, sound like something recognisable, but there is an extra thrill in making something brand new and surprising. The students should be given licence to experiment and to travel creatively towards new musical horizons.

4) **Harmony and counterpoint are the core building blocks**
As suggested above, once 'harmony' is liberated from its accompanying role to 'melody' a whole new vista can open up. And when the student realises that 'chords' can have more than three pitches, or need not connect to major or minor keys, then the compositional imagination can run riot!

Also, 'counterpoint' can mean many things. Some associate the word with the dusty, academic study of older styles. Knowing how Bach imagined his disparate lines in his fugues and two- and three-part inventions is important, of course. As is the acquirement of insight into how even earlier composers put line against line in Motets and Masses. But there are other definitions of musical complexity that can aid the students' musical vision. What about rhythm against rhythm? Pulse against pulse? Tonality against tonality? Modality against modality? Tempo against tempo? What happens when you put one kind of music up against another and play them together?! The class might benefit from listening to some of the original 'mash-ups' by the American composer Charles Ives, such as *The Unanswered Question* or *Central Park in the Dark*.

5) **The principles are the same when working in traditional tonality and atonality**
Sometimes it's difficult or unnecessary to feel the centre or core of tonality in a piece of music. In the early 20th century some composers took their tonalities in such a direction that it became impossible to locate the 'key' in any traditional sense. A lot of this 'atonal' music found a natural home in film scores from the 1930s onwards. Some say that atonal music found its most idiomatic context in the world of film. Many film watchers have no issue with this strange music accompanying their favourite, tense on-screen dramas, but in the concert hall some listeners find the atonal experience strange. But it is this very strangeness which can excite and motivate composers, and young composers especially should feel free to explore these directions too. The fundamentals that one finds in tonal music are the same in atonality too. Making an unusual, angular melody out of a jumbled range of pitches can take the music in fantastic unexplored directions. And making harmony out of non-traditional note groups can be truly liberating.

6) **Music is the ultimate tool for discrete self-expression**
Music communicates beyond word and image and is therefore a more mysterious art form than literature and the visual arts. We live in a world dominated by the visual and the verbal and music seems to speak of the unknown and the deep in ways that can seem unusual and beyond the immediate. This is its strength. And young musicians can find that they are able to 'speak' or 'paint' more fluently in sound sculptures than in the more normative modes of expression. Composing can truly be a liberating form of self-expression that can impact greatly on the lives of the individuals involved. Compose alongside your students whenever you can.

7) **Break the rules – make up your own**
Although composers can benefit from the study of basic principles in composition such as traditional harmony and counterpoint, they should feel that they are always given licence to go beyond the 'rules'. This has always been the case, certainly since the early 19th century in classical music, and maybe even before. The 20th century opened up entirely new ways of thinking about composition. Students should enjoy the freedom that is available to them.

8) **Encourage analysis of the music the students are playing**
Being able to look closely and reflectively at any piece of music will be of enormous help to a young composer. They should begin with the music that they themselves perform. It can be helpful to look with new eyes and new ears at the most familiar music. And the most helpful questions the young analyst can ask – Why is the composer doing this? What technical devices is he/she deploying? How does the music hold together structurally? What does this music make me feel? What is the mood of this music and how is it achieved? etc.

9) **It's a didactic process that takes time**
Like all artistic forms, the composition of music needs to be worked at. It can lead to a lifetime of creative work for some of us. But even in the short term, students should develop a patience for learning. The creative juices may not flow immediately and slow, reflective analytical thought and practice will get things going in due course.